The Art of
Edward Wesson

RON RANSON

The Art of
Edward Wesson

RON RANSON

David & Charles

Acknowledgements

Frontispiece:
THE MOORING (Watercolour)
I love this painting, its got so much sparkle, movement and contrast which epitomises Ted's best work. The water has been handled with his usual aplomb, and he's allowed the whiteness of the paper to play its own part in the picture. While the painting is mostly cool greens and blues, the odd touches of red provide contrasting warmth.

A DAVID & CHARLES BOOK

First published in the UK in 1993
First paperback edition 2004
Reprinted 2005

Text copyright © Ron Ranson 1993, 2004
Illustrations copyright © C. E. Wesson 1993, 2004

Ron Ranson has asserted his right to be identified as author of this work in accordance with the Copyright, Designs and Patents Act, 1988.

A catalogue record for this book is available from the British Library.

ISBN 0 7153 1700 8

Typeset by ABM Typographics Ltd
Printed in Singapore by KHL Printing Co Pte Ltd
for David & Charles
Brunel House   Newton Abbot   Devon

Visit our website at www.davidandcharles.co.uk

David & Charles books are available from all good bookshops; alternatively you can contact our Orderline on (0)1626 334555 or write to us at FREEPOST EX2 110, David & Charles Direct, Newton Abbot, TQ12 4ZZ (no stamp required UK mainland).

I've loved doing this book because of the enthusiasm of everyone I approached, particularly Mrs Wesson. Not only has she gone to endless trouble finding material for me, but she also made sure that while I was with her I never went hungry! My thanks are due to Peter Geiringer for allowing me to use pictures from his collection, and to Peter Sherwood and Stephen Crawley for their photography.

I also received scores of offers of paintings from Wesson fans all over the country, which owing to lack of space, I was unable to use. I do hope, however, that they enjoy the finished book.

Finally, I'd like to thank Ann Mills for her invaluable help in the preparation of this book, and Jenny Hickey who did all the typing from my indecipherable script.

With regard to the sizes of the paintings in this book, as most of them are scattered all around the country, or even the world, it hasn't been possible to obtain the dimensions of the oils. However, nearly all of the watercolours were done on half-imperial sheets, so the actual picture sizes because of Wesson's frame were about 13 × 20½in.

Contents

Introduction

During the years that I have been writing painting instruction books, and later books about other artists and their methods, one name has cropped up over and over again. Everyone, including my publishers, wanted to know, 'When are you going to do a book on Edward Wesson?' Now, no one is a bigger fan of his than I am, but what made me hesitate was not the writing, but the thought of having to scour the country trying to find his work in hundreds of homes, and then to photograph it on their walls, through glass, to a very high standard.

After a lot of thought, I decided to put a very small three-line ad in the personal column of the *Leisure Painter* to the effect that I was contemplating writing a book on Edward Wesson and would like to hear from owners of his paintings willing to help. I expected half a dozen replies, but was deluged with letters which continued to arrive for months afterwards. I honestly can't think of any other artist, living or dead, who could create such downright affection. He was not a remote figure whom people admired from afar. Once you'd met him, you

regarded him as a friend. Personally, I don't think of him as Edward Wesson, RI, but as Ted, and that's what I intend to call him in the rest of this book, not disrespectfully, but with my own 'downright affection'.

I went to see his wife, Dickie, at their home in Guildford. She was her usual charming self, bright as a button, and delighted that someone was at last going to do a book about Ted. What I didn't expect though, was that she would have four, full slide carousels of Ted's paintings. We went into the garage that had been Ted's studio for many years (incidentally, she told me he even went in there on

Christmas mornings to paint!), and as I sat excitedly looking at literally hundreds of slides, I realised that this would be my main source of material for the book. The only snag was that they had been shown to countless art societies over the years, and many of them had got the odd splash of paint on them. Ted would be the first to admit he was not the most meticulous man when he had a paintbrush in his hand! Still, what's the occasional splash among friends?

Ted claimed that he and his twin brother, Philip could both call themselves Edwardians, because they were born a few days before the

ST IVES, HUNTINGDON (Watercolour)
I love the subtlety of the various greys and browns in this painting. Although the colours are subdued, there is a very warm, sunny quality. I remember seeing it in the RI exhibition, and was immediately drawn towards it – unfortunately, it already had a red 'sold' sticker on it!

old King died in 1910. His father, a true cockney, was born within the sound of Bow Bells, and was from a timber-merchant family. His mother's family made lifts for big houses and hospitals.

At grammar school, Ted was much more distinguished at sport than as a scholar. He remembered himself as 'an idle fellow' at lessons, but captained the school's Rugby XV. He managed to avoid the disgrace of failing matriculation by finding a job, with his father's help, in textiles, while his twin brother Phil stayed on another year, took his exams and went into shipping.

Ted worked diligently at his job, but around 1930 at the age of 20, he developed an urge to paint, and began to fill his spare time with sketches made in nearby Greenwich Park. So began a course which was to bring him so much fun and reward for the rest of his life. From the park, he progressed to the river, with its shipping and barges on the foreshore – then to skies and wide open landscapes. The main theme was to develop painting in the field in the purest and simplest form.

During the early 1930s, he worked for the textile firm in the City. Times were hard and he supplemented his income by holding down an appointment as organist in a small church near Tower Bridge – using his additional talent in music. This also continued to be part of his life. In 1933 he met his future wife 'Dickie', when they both appeared in a big night pageant in Greenwich. But let me explain how the lifelong love of Ted's life, christened Caroline Elizabeth, got her nickname. Her brother was seven when she was born, and not overjoyed about the new arrival. His first comment on viewing her, was that she looked more like a bird than a baby – hence 'Dickie'. The name stuck and from then on she was never called anything else by her family.

About this time, he met Mr L.S.M. Prince who was then principal of the art department at Woolwich Polytechnic. After seeing the young man's work, he advised him to continue doing his own thing, as he felt that training might undo much that Ted had already achieved and might even spoil him. Ted was ever afterwards grateful for this advice, and continued on his own. He was, however, influenced by such artists as E. W. Haslehust, Adrian Hill and Adrian Bury, who he felt could show him so much about direct, pure watercolour.

Ted and Dickie were married in December 1937, and as war clouds gathered, he joined as a Territorial, the Heavy Anti-Aircraft Regiment of the Honourable Artillery Company. Once war was declared, he spent his time on various sites around London until he was sent off to OCTU (Officer Cadet Training Unit) in May 1940.

On his third wedding anniversary in December 1940, he sailed from Liverpool for Egypt, and was not to see Dickie again until May 1945 – a long time to be away. As Ted said afterwards, one of the good things about the war was that he was posted to Suez, where he was able to paint in his spare time, and

Edward Wesson in his studio.

Dickie managed to mail him *The Artist* magazine regularly, as well as colours as he needed them. In Port Said he even played the organ in the church.

In 1943, he was involved in the invasion of Sicily, and after the dust of battle settled, he was invited to play the organ at a mass for the troops – probably the first Englishman to play for a service in Europe before the actual liberation. As the theatre of war moved up into Italy, Ted went with it, and at Pisa he met Ascarnio Tealdi, a prominent Tuscan painter who was acting as an interpreter. They established a great rapport, and Ted became fascinated by oil painting perhaps because Tealdi made it look so easy. When he left Pisa for home, he was determined to try his hand at the medium; conversely, he left the Italian dabbling in watercolour.

On being demobbed, the Wessons still had their problems. Their little house in Petts Wood had been destroyed by a flying bomb in 1944 (fortunately Dickie was away working in Stourport on Severn). They had to share a requisitioned house until they managed to get the house rebuilt, and what was left of the furniture repaired in 1947.

Once they settled down together again, Ted began to think about painting once more. He had sold quite a few of his pictures on the boat coming home, which gave him ideas, and started him thinking. Ted was introduced to Sidney Weeks, who after seeing Ted's work, advised him of galleries where he could submit his paintings. Ted also got in touch with the RI (Royal Institute of Painters in Watercolour), and here he met the Secretary, Reggie Blackmore, who was tremendously helpful. There was a joint exhibition of RI, RP (Royal Society of Portrait Painters) and ROI (Royal Institute of Oil Painters) at Burlington House (the RI Gallery in Piccadilly was out of action because of war damage). Although the taking-in day had passed, Blackmore managed to smuggle in three of Ted's paintings before the selection committee met. All three were hung.

This exhibition was like the opening of an Aladdin's cave for Ted, and he became acquainted with the works of many of the very best watercolour artists of the day such as Arthur Burgess, Frank H. Mason, Fred Taylor, Frank Sherwin, Raymond Sheppard, Jack Merriott, Claud Buckle, Norman Wilkinson and Rowland Hilder. Faced with such a feast of excellent and competent work, Ted resolved that he would try to carry on the tradition, at the same time aiming to loosen up and simplify what these fine men had so eloquently shown him.

By this time he'd returned to his job in the City, but tried to paint as much as he could – slipping down to the river between the city bridges for an hour or so, and at the same time following the exhibition scene in the West End. He learned to take in facts quickly, and paint quickly, something that he found invaluable ever after. He began to realise that the best results in watercolour were obtained when he had to work at speed. This meant of necessity that all detail had to be left out because of the limited time available.

In the mid-fifties, Ted was invited to join the Wapping Group of Artists, a prestigious group who were interested in painting the Thames. They had their headquarters at the famous Prospect of Whitby pub, and painted the tidal waters from Teddington to Whit-

stable. They limited their membership to twenty-six and included some of the top artists in the country.

During this time, the business in the City was not good, and his firm was forced to ask the staff to take a thirty per cent cut in their salaries. It was just as well, therefore, that some commissions for paintings started to come in. British Rail invited him to do posters for them, and Ted completed fifteen before Dr Beeching stamped on all pictorial poster work. However when one door closes, another one opens; Post Office Savings Banks started a series of imperial-sized posters of their branches, and Ted was asked to participate along with many other artists such as Jack Merriott, Leonard Squirrel, Angus Rands and Claud Muncaster. Apart from some local ones in Surrey they asked him to look out for post offices in the wilds of Scotland. One of these was a shack on the shores of the Kyle of Tongue. It seemed such an unlikely place, that Ted had first to satisfy himself that it really was an office, by drawing some money out of the PO Bank before he painted it!

Ted also got lots of private commissions to paint peoples' homes and gardens; some were attractive and a pleasure to do, but many were extremely tiresome. Owners wanted wisteria added, bulbs and aubretias in the rockeries, doors and windows opened and deck-chairs added. Having done some of this type of work in the past, I know the frustrations; because the owners are not painters, they know none of the limitations, and demand impossible angles and lighting.

Ted's 'proper' business entailed a lot of travelling in France and Belgium, and these continental journeys gave him more subject matter for his paintings. He always managed

The Post Office at CRINAN, LOCHGILPHEAD ARGYLL   From a painting by Edward Wesson R.I., R.B.A., R.S.M.

 Wherever you go ... there is a branch of the
NATIONAL SAVINGS BANK
... at the Post Office

Above is one of the many posters that Ted painted for the Post Office Savings Bank.

to arrange his continental trips so that he had the weekend to paint at home in Gomshall. He had bought a bungalow situated in a valley where there was all the subject matter he wanted just outside the door. All this meant that he was able to fill his spot at the RI, have shows at the Reid Gallery whenever they invited him, as well as having regular exhibitions at the Gordon Gallery in Wimbledon.

He also began writing articles in the *The Artist* magazine, and later in the *Leisure Painter*, so he was able to express his own theories and ideas on painting, to an ever-growing audience. It was through *The Artist* magazine, too, that from the late 1950s onwards, he was to become involved with tutoring painting holidays, both in England and on the Continent.

They stayed in their bungalow at Gomshall for nine years. However it wasn't ideal as Ted

11

had no studio and had to make do with a bench at the end of the garage. In 1967 they moved to Pilgrim Cottage in Guildford, which was a great improvement, as there was an old coach-house in the yard – the house dated from 1895 – and this was to be Ted's studio thereafter.

It was at this time that Ted began to arrange his own watercolour courses in various parts of the country, in places such as the Albion Hotel at Freshwater on the Isle of Wight, and Bassenthwaite in the Lake District, among many other locations. Dickie went with him on most of the trips, perhaps to protect him from his adoring public and also to prevent him from giving his paintings away at ridiculous prices. She felt, quite rightly, that he didn't charge nearly enough for his work. On one of his courses, I was offered a selection of his half-imperial watercolours at just £10 each – I bought four, which I'm still proud to exhibit on my walls.

Throughout his life, Ted smoked incessantly. Even in his forties, suffering from hardened arteries in his leg, he ignored the advice given to him to give it up, and in his sixties he was still a sixty-a-day man. In 1977, he suffered his first coronary, almost certainly brought on by the smoking. Even then, in hospital, he bribed the nurses to buy him cigarettes. He had another coronary in 1982; in April 1983, while still working, he became seriously ill. This time there was no recovery; Ted died on 5 September.

This was a terrible time for Dickie as she was also suffering from cancer of the breast, and to quote her directly, 'didn't know which of us was going to pop off first'. Happily, Dickie recovered, and is now living contentedly in her lovely new home in Rustington, still surrounded by Ted's paintings.

The Wesson Philosophy

When a colleague asked Ted Wesson if he had written a book, as he'd be interested to know what Ted's philosophy was, Ted, in his usual nonchalant way, said he'd always been too busy to bother with philosophy. The friend retorted, 'That's as good a philosophy as any!' However, if you were to substitute the word 'philosophy' with 'strong convictions' or 'firm unshakeable beliefs', then Ted had them in full. He was completely outspoken and fearless in his opinions about the craft of painting, or as he himself put it 'what is and what is not "on" in art'.

Ted was self-taught, and because of this always felt that he was a bit on the fringe of things – though this never really bothered him. Indeed he felt it had bred in him a feeling of freedom, which allowed him to do his own thing without being hidebound by theory, or the dictates of the pundits. Being self-taught myself, I share his feelings exactly; there is a certain satisfaction in being a rebel. Ted quotes Dunlop, who wrote in his book *Landscape Painting*, that art schools do not produce artists, but those who can apply art to given ends. Nevertheless, there is very definite value in attending art school – the opportunity of working with other students and the criticism of each other's work, things that really matter in the life of a student. Ted felt he had missed these and it explains why he always felt himself to be rather in the wilderness.

Dunlop also said, 'To go one's way without help of art schools and fellow students is the really hard way, and probably best for

those with enough originality and toughness of character to become creative artists with a personal vision of their own so unique that they'd be the ones to impress themselves on future generations'. This particularly applies to landscape painters as there is no good way of teaching landscape art in schools. Ted found that pupils were constantly coming to him complaining that no one in art schools could show them how to paint a landscape. They were delighted to find a tutor who would demonstrate to them, and show them what they wanted to see.

So what were these strong opinions he held? First and foremost was his dedication to 'purity' in watercolour. Whenever he was asked what medium he preferred, he always said 'When it comes off, there's nothing like a good watercolour'. He felt it had a unique quality, the key being the paper itself. The process of painting should disturb the surface of the paper as little as possible; pushing the paint around and manipulating it destroys its magic – he was a traditionalist, and proud of it.

He viewed with undisguised disdain those artists who threw water, grit or salt at their work, distancing himself from what he termed 'Americanism' – the use of masking fluid, body colour and scraping-out techniques. These he felt were just exercises on the studio bench. He said he preferred to let the other chaps play around with their cameras, wax and billposters' buckets as long as he was allowed to continue in his corner of the field to look at the wonders of things round him. He felt that Constable, Bonnington, Manet and Bawden were more than enough inspiration for him, and helped to keep his feet firmly on the ground.

He quoted John Singer Sargent, that emi-nent and reclusive master watercolourist who ignored current affairs and trends, even refusing to read any daily newspapers. He remained loyal to the Impressionists, feeling that post-impressionism was only an inven-tion of the sharper art dealers of the day. Ted was also happy to stay with the traditional, and he felt that much of our so-called modern art was just a result of exploitation by the present day unscrupulous dealers, and some-thing that critics enjoyed curling their tongues round.

To Ted, a lot of what was going on in art seemed topsy-turvy. He felt the medium of watercolour must be allowed to have its own way; it needed to flow easily otherwise it wasn't good watercolour, and if we wanted it to stay where we put it, why not use a more static medium, like pastel or oil. He couldn't therefore, for the life of him, understand why acrylics should come under the heading of watercolour. 'Someone may say they are water-based, but so is a pile of bricks, so why shouldn't the bricks at the Tate be hung with the watercolours?'

He could never understand who made the rules about what is good in art, and why folk were looked on as Philistines if they didn't concur. There were things about modern art that Ted couldn't tolerate and what was more he was very happy to feel that way. He put this down to being a non-conformist. Ted couldn't stand pompous people and all those who struck poses. Many of them, he felt, were products of our art schools, who had never experienced the sheer joy of painting in the field. He attended as few exhibitions as possible mainly to avoid being embarrassed by work he might be asked to comment on. Ted was never one to suffer fools gladly – or silently!

The French Polisher's mop, which helped to give Ted's paintings their loose and distinctive style.

Watercolour Painting

Before getting down to specifics of Ted's equipment and techniques in watercolour, let's explore his views on the subject.

He said that a medium such as watercolour must have its limitations. For instance, it cannot be pushed about and worked on without losing what he considered its main quality – freshness and transparency. 'In order to get over the problem, we need to simplify the subject in front of us so that there won't be the necessity for any overworking or fiddling. A range of hills in the distance must be captured in one brush stroke. Clumps of trees must be treated as masses and put down in their respective correct tones. Of course some definition will have to be added so that the mass will have meaning, but these additions will not be so much painting as drawing with a brush.'

He felt that the most important thing was the paper itself, and that we must make very good use of it by trying to lay all our washes on to it once only. This makes for a luminosity which we don't find in any other medium, and if we can actually leave parts of the paper untouched in certain circumstances, it will give a natural sparkle to passages which no amount of chinese white could achieve. He never did like using white paint and always discouraged it in his students.

He said that he often stood before a virgin sheet of his Bockingford paper and thought that in that state it was probably the best watercolour he would ever produce, and would then proceed to spoil it by adding colour to it. How he applied this colour would determine whether the work would be good or bad: 'A good watercolour in my opinion, is a happy marriage between paper and colour. It's only where we find we have to tinker about afterwards adding a bit here and a bit there, and in the process gradually obliterating the loveliness of the paper, that we will all know we've failed.'

As I said, the paper itself was of the utmost importance to Ted. He stressed that everyone needed to find a paper which they personally enjoyed using, and that suited their particular taste. There are hundreds of papers to choose from with widely different surfaces and prices. Once a suitable paper has been found, however, people tend to stick loyally to it, in spite of all newcomers. Ted's paper was Bockingford. When he first chose it back in the 1950s the heaviest weight obtainable was 140lb, thick enough for most people, including myself – I use it constantly.

However, Ted needed to find a weight that wouldn't waver or buckle in extreme conditions of cold or damp air.

Lunching one day in the early 1960s with Mr Remé Green of Barcham Green who made the paper, he discussed his problem. Mr Green promptly offered to make 1,000 sheets of 200lb for him to see if he liked it. Ted took 250 sheets as a starter and found it ideal. However, he hesitated to tell Green in case he wanted him to take the other 750 then and there. He needn't have worried as Rowneys bought the rest, and Barcham Green were making another five tons of it. Ted used it from then on, and smugly liked to think of it as *his* paper.

Now to his colours. He was always a little reluctant to disclose these as he felt his own choice was not important to anyone else. What was important was that there were only eight of them. He felt the fewer colours were used, the more quickly would their possibilities be understood. The colours were in fact winsor blue, ultramarine, cobalt, burnt umber, burnt sienna, raw sienna, light red and warm winsor yellow. To people who thought a larger range would be needed in other parts of the world, he said that apart from specific colours seen locally in flower arrangements, he found that everything he saw could be obtained from his little range, and he had painted in such places as diverse as the British Isles, South Africa, the Near East and the Mediterranean.

In Britain the atmosphere softens the colours off, and nothing is quite as it comes straight from the tube. All the distant blues need 'greying off' with a brown or light red, and warmer colours need tempering with one of the blues to give the look produced by our weather and climate. However, the Mediterranean does not need this mellowing and the colours can be used straight from the tube – burnt sienna for the roof tiles and perhaps pure Winsor blue for the sea.

Now to the brush, which I believe helped to give Ted's paintings such a fluid feeling. It was the polisher's mop, a brush he found in France made of squirrel hair and bound with wire. It was comparatively floppy when wet, as opposed to a springy sable most watercolourists use. Ted used it with tremendous confidence and aplomb and virtually made it his own. He also used a couple of small sables for branches and rigging.

Another item which Ted devised himself, and which gave his work an individual look, was a frame to hold the sheets of 200lb Bockingford. It consisted of a sheet of hardboard cut to take a half-imperial size paper, and another cut to form a frame. The two were hinged with tape and clipped together at the other end with spring clips which gave an opening of approximately 19×13in. It resulted in a distinctive deckle-edge look to all Ted's work which was very attractive. If you're lucky enough to have one of Ted's paintings, look for it. Of course, hundreds of his students copied his idea too.

When friends asked him where he found his subjects, he said it was rather that the subjects found him. He meant that he was governed by an appreciation of his own limitations and only a few of the many possible subjects seemed to recommend themselves to him. He said that on journeys, Dickie might slow down the car and suggest some grand panorama, but he knew it would be too much for him, especially in watercolour. A little further on he'd ask her to slow down and park by a hedge because he'd seen a single, well-lit tree or a gate, which with luck he felt he'd capture to the possible envy of his friends. There are many times when we all try for the really impossible. However, Ted felt there was a certain merit in not always setting one's sights too high, rather sometimes being content with doing simple things, with beauty and understanding.

Line and Wash Painting

This was a variation of Ted's watercolour technique. It was a very attractive method of showing detail and texture in architectural subjects, for example (see pages 41 and 111). He found there was a great demand for this type of painting from him, probably because many purchasers liked to see more detail than he would normally consider essential. Moreover, it did enable the artist to show more easily the textures in trees, trunks and branches and the various surfaces in buildings and roofs.

Ted was always amused that this method was so popular with his buyers because he felt, provided the artist could draw, it was much easier than pure watercolour ever could be. Nevertheless, in the hands of an expert such as Rowland Hilder this method could be used to produce absolute masterpieces.

However, with characteristic individualism, Ted hardly ever used a conventional pen. He wanted something which would produce a broader, freer line. He normally used a twig from a nearby hedge or a matchstick stuck into the end of a garden cane. The cane acted as a penholder and the matchstick was

about the softest wood for the purpose. Once, while I was with him on a course, however, I remember he'd gone on to sharpened ice-lolly sticks, saying gleefully that the beauty of it all was that you didn't have to buy them – they could be had by searching in any gutter or waste bin.

He used waterproof black ink with a limited palette of four colours, burnt umber, burnt sienna, raw sienna and also Payne's grey which he substituted for his three normal blues because he felt it worked better with the ink. He always tried with this technique not to use pencil first but to go straight in with ink. He felt that inking over a pencil drawing was not much more than tracing which would result in the loss of character or 'handwriting'. He did however admit that this method was a risky business.

He also enjoyed the soft nature of the 'pen' strokes which as the ink soaked into the wood, gave a look of charcoal drawing and a

quality and texture much more easy on the eye than lines from a hard steel nib. You'll find many examples of this quality among the many sketches scattered about this section.

Oil Painting

For Ted, oils seemed so much easier than watercolour. So much so that he always felt there must be some catch – but he never found out what it was! In fact he always had more success with his oils than with his watercolours at the Royal Academy. Although he submitted watercolours for many years, they were accepted but never hung.

His first two articles in *The Artist* were on painting in oils, and after they were published Ted wrote to the editor and told him he was really a watercolourist, having been elected to the RI eight years previously. He was then

asked to do a series on watercolour which began a long and happy connection with both *The Artist* and subsequently the *Leisure Painter*.

He worked out a system of painting in oils that suited him perfectly for working quickly on the spot. This idea came to him while studying Constable's smaller panels in the Tate Gallery. These he found more sparkling and spontaneous than the larger, more formal works and through which he could see the warm under-colour of the prepared ground. He realised that by preparing his own panels with a similar warm tint, it would give him a good start for a work which could be accomplished within two hours or so. On previously prepared board, he dotted about the board a mixture of ultramarine and burnt umber, each straight from the tube, and then worked over it with a rag soaked in turpentine. This gave a warm but subdued ground on which to paint.

His colours were very similar to the ones he used in watercolour, with a few exceptions. The list was: Winsor blue, ultramarine, cobalt, burnt umber, burnt sienna, yellow ochre, Winsor lemon, cadmium scarlet plus titanium white. As to brushes, he felt three were sufficient. He used a 2in decorator's brush for broadly rubbing in the main areas, a No 9 or 10 for carrying the work further and a No 6 for final detail such as branches and windows.

His 'drill' was to split his time into two periods of one hour each. During the first hour he composed the subject, followed by a rough rubbing-in of the approximate colours and tones in very thin colour. The only medium he used was turpentine (not white spirit). He avoided white at this stage because he felt that it easily became 'chalky' – usually the main mistake of the amateur. If white is left alone for as long as possible there is less risk of this. The original toned ground enabled him to achieve a lot in the first hour. Then after a few minutes' break the rubbing-in had dried out sufficiently because of the turpentine. He could then add good fat paint without it sliding about all over the place; he never added any extra oil, as he felt there was enough already in the paint. This process took up the second hour and the painting was finished.

Teaching

Ted Wesson was a tireless and inspiring teacher. He loved the game, and honestly felt he got as much out of it as he was able to put in. He said the feeling that he'd been able to pass on something to others gave him a sense of satisfaction hard to put into words. He had a punishing schedule, doing about twelve weeks of tutoring in the summer months, and scores of lecture/demonstrating evenings throughout the year. These talks were usually at art societies scattered all over the country from Plymouth to Carlisle, and as his reputation as a humorous and exciting demonstrator grew, so did the size of his audiences. The venues were always packed to capacity.

Even when he was still working full time at his business activities in the fifties, he began to travel around widely to lecture, and to conduct weekend courses. He was beginning to burn the candle at both ends, and he said his

poor family didn't see much of him at that time. However, he began to earn a reasonable income from these activities, and he also began tutoring several painting holidays for *The Artist* magazine, by giving up his own holiday time.

Gradually, Ted began to feel that he might make as much money from art as he had been earning from business, so he decided to take the plunge. He gave up his regular job, and became a full-time professional artist. In fact, in the first year after the break was made, he earned twice as much as he previously had from the two incomes put together.

Art societies now engaged him to work whole weeks for them, and he began to organise courses on his own. Thus began an annual series of weeks in places like Corfe Castle, Woburn, Yarmouth in the Isle of Wight, Rye, Walberswick, Chichester and of course Dinton, where the warden, Group Captain John Smither asked him to do several weeks. These were stepped up by the succeeding warden, Squadron Leader Peter Jones, and for years afterwards, Ted did five weeks there annually.

Dinton is very much part of the Wesson legend. Philipps House in the village of Dinton is a huge and very distinguished country mansion, in its own parkland. It was originally called Dinton Park and was built for the Wymondham family. Later it was owned by a Mr Philipps who eventually handed it over to the National Trust and the YMCA, seemingly to house twenty ladies of perfect virtue. Apparently the supply of such ladies ran out and they were forced to run painting courses to help it to pay its way. Sympathetically restored over the years, the original library, furniture and pictures are still there to be enjoyed.

On a personal note, I often tried to join one of Ted's courses there, but never managed to get in. It always seemed full of adoring lady students who booked from course to course. Now, however, I know and love the place well, as I am one of the many tutors who teach painting there, year after year.

Many of the mature ladies who were his regulars he would refer to affectionately as his 'old trouts'. However, in his own mind, he always thought of all his pupils as falling into three categories. Firstly, there were those such as teachers, architects, and 'go-getters',

This sensitive portrait was drawn by Juliet Pannett PS, FRSA, while on one of Ted's courses at Walberswick. It was a wet day, and she suggested that she should do a portrait demonstration with Ted as sitter.

who came eagerly to learn the trade and went away after a year or two to do their own thing. Secondly, there were those who came back regularly, year after year, knowing they just wanted to improve their painting, and kept on coming to form the backbone of the

18

Dinton courses. Finally, there were the few (bless them) who seemed to come, as he put it, 'just for the beer'. They obviously enjoyed the house and the atmosphere and painted only when they felt they must. Whatever the mix, Ted's gruff humour and the many asides, especially during the demonstrations, meant that the atmosphere was always relaxed and light-hearted.

I remember finally managing to join Ted for a painting week at Walberswick in East Anglia, where I also had the pleasure of meeting Dickie for the first time. We painted along the river bank with its distinctive huts. The painting on page 48 brings memories flooding back. Inevitably, we had a wet afternoon and Ted took the opportunity of doing one of his flower demonstrations in the village hall. He popped a few red and white roses into an old jamjar, seemingly carelessly, but in reality, much thought was given to the counterchange of the white flowers against the dark foliage and the red ones against the light background. He attacked the painting with light-hearted gusto, using his famous polisher's mop. The roses were just as he liked them, open and fully blown, rather than tight buds. He

WINTER FEED IN WYLYE VALLEY
(Watercolour)

Ted said about this picture, that he always enjoyed the scene when there was an 'r' in the month, as from September to April, the colours were gradually changing. He also said, 'Although a winter scene, I felt there was much colour here. The sky was a warm peach draped in a mid-morning mist, and the field and the scrub at the base of the trees, warm and full in the winter sunshine.'

felt that these had a freedom about the shape and a quality of light that such fully blown flowers seem to acquire just before they fade forever.

That afternoon was so enjoyable, as indeed was the whole week with Ted. Such was the magical attraction of his classes, that they always seemed to be fully booked, no matter how many he had per year.

There were always plenty of stories that went the rounds among his students and ex-students about his gruff and sometimes outrageous humour, which was mostly put over with a completely straight face. It was the same off-hand humour as used by that famous comedy actor, Fred Emney. Ted's own explanation of his love of teaching was typical of him. Firstly, he said that he was never subtle enough to hide what little knowledge he'd acquired, and that he'd also been blessed with a clowning mentality, enabling him to make a kind of 'music-hall act' out of it all. He always hoped he had amused more people than he had offended. He needn't have worried – his fan club must have numbered thousands, and what is more, it still does.

He was often asked whether it was in order to copy another artist's work. He always said 'Why on earth not?' He had no hesitation at all, on a wet day, in offering sketches of his own for copying by the students. He felt that if they, as individuals, had anything at all to say, it wouldn't be long before they were saying it in their own language.

He felt that the amateur needed to see the teacher at work, discussing together the problems as they arose. Something rubbed off in each session and they could absorb more each time they jointly came into contact with nature. He also felt that pupils should be

given as much encouragement as possible. Many were often ready to tear up their work just at the point where they should be pressing on a bit further to see a way of resolving all the problems. He felt that a pat on the shoulder had often saved a little gem for posterity. How wise he was.

I remember a few years ago talking to John Blockley, RI, an artist for whom I've a great respect. Talking about my own future, John said 'you've got to make up your mind whether you're going to be an artist or a teacher'. This was logical, like choosing to be either a piano teacher or a concert pianist. I decided after some heartsearching that I could communicate better than I could paint!

Ted Wesson, however, had the ability and good humour to become a legend with feet in both camps, and thousands will remember Ted with huge affection and loyalty, whether they own his pictures or have been taught by him. The author feels very privileged to have enjoyed both and hopes that this book will play its small part in perpetuating his memory.

NORFOLK, WELLS-NEXT-THE-SEA
(Watercolour)

This is such a gloriously sunny picture, it makes you want to smile. Your eye is drawn immediately to the white end-wall, just off-centre, with its two dark figures, counterchanged against it. Notice how the other two figures have light clothes just in the right place. The house is given more prominence by the strong contrast and the brightness of the adjacent roof.

CRICKET AT TAUNTON (Watercolour)

It's surprising how Ted has managed to convey so much of the atmosphere of a cricket match, with such economy and freshness. The distinctive profile of Taunton has also been portrayed in the same loose, and yet satisfying way. Notice how the sight-screen is counterchanged against the dark pavilion.

THAMES AT TOWER BRIDGE
(Watercolour)

A complete change of light and atmosphere here. Notice how the sunlit sparkle on the river is directly behind the dark tug to give it even more drama. Tower Bridge can be a bit of a cliché – but not in this picture.

SKYE (Watercolour)

One of Ted's characteristically simple scenes. Again, his use of cool colours in the background, and warm in the foreground to gain depth, is a good lesson to all aspiring watercolourists. Look how simply he's treated the water, avoiding the temptation to fuss it.

SNOW ON THE RIVER (Watercolour)
This is a classic Wesson winter scene, with its stillness and calm. The reflections are handled with masterly simplicity, and the warm, golden sky contrasts well with the cold greys of the winter trees.

23

BASSENTHWAITE VILLAGE, CUMBRIA
(Line and wash)

The free line-work in this painting immediately points to Ted's use of the sharpened matchstick (much more creative than a pen). Whilst the background is very subdued, there is lots of contrast and counterchange in the foreground buildings. The main tree is a strong vertical element in an otherwise horizontal picture. The colours are restricted as always in this line and wash work.

BLACKWATER FOOT, ARRAN (Oils)
There is a strength and vitality about this
painting. It looks as though a solitary ray of
sunlight has hit the cottage and beach in an
otherwise stormy atmosphere. Ted has left us in
no doubt about the focal point – the cottage
with its contrasting black door.

PAPER MILL COTTAGES, BURNESIDE,
CUMBRIA (Watercolour)
*Basically a straightforward row of cottages,
but by using reflections Ted has made a very
interesting picture from it. The light in the sky
throws up the varied roof line, accentuated by
the chimney pots. It's interesting to see his
treatment of the windows and the way he has
left so many whites.*

CHRYSANTHEMUMS (Oils)

Here there is a definite colour combination of orange and grey, punctuated by the whites, the subdued grey accentuating the warm glow of the flowers. Notice too, how the surrounding dark foliage is also used to pick out the whites. The fallen petals on the table add interest.

EAST COAST BEACH (Oils)
One of the delightful things about this simple picture is the strong textural quality of the paint itself; you can almost feel how Ted enjoyed himself. Notice how the central object, the lighthouse, is just off-centre, vertically and horizontally.

BRANCASTER STAITHE (Watercolour)
I love this picture, there's lots packed into it, yet it retains a strong sense of unity. The white boat, combined with the bright red roofs, is visually exciting, and you can almost feel the warmth of a sunny, summer day.

SHADOWS ON A SNOWY BANK
(Watercolour)
Although this painting provides a complete change of mood and atmosphere from the one opposite, there is a similarity in the fact that all the 'action' takes place on one horizontal level. While it is a basically cool picture, there are some effective, and necessary, touches of warmth too.

ST MARY'S, BRISTOL (Oils)
This really is a beautiful painting. Although Ted, among other artists, has tackled the same subject in various mediums, this one in oils must be one of the most successful. The softness of the sky emphasises the crisp quality of the buildings and boats.

GUILDFORD CATHEDRAL FROM MERROW DOWNS (Watercolour)
This is a lesson in simplicity – a limited palette, and lots of uncluttered space, yet the whole thing conveys so much atmosphere. Notice how the footprints take the eye through the snow to the main object of interest, the distant tower. Again, you will notice the church steeple is just off-centre.

34

HEYBRIDGE BASIN (Watercolour)
This was a good exercise in presenting the white of the paper where it was needed – Ted always refused to resort to chinese white. He managed to capture the scene on a very still afternoon at high tide, and by working at speed, had it all down before there was any appreciable change in the water level.

THE "GRAPES"
LIMEHOUSE

FLOWER STUDY (Oils)

The richness of texture and colour here is exciting. It's worth comparing this with the chrysanthemums on page 28. Ted has used a wide variety of colours which complement each other, and the flowers have been organised to provide maximum interest.

CORFE CASTLE (Watercolour)

Another all-time favourite for artists, and Ted has painted this scene many times, often from different aspects. There's a nice pattern of light and shade here, even the foreground field, with its strong contrast of sunshine and shadow, adds excitement and depth.

ROCHESTER, KENT (Watercolour)
*With a restrained palette, Ted has managed to
convey the atmosphere of this busy port, with a
minimum of detail, relying on the profile and
counterchange for effect. Notice how simply
he's treated the distant hill, with just one flat
wash. The picture is made more interesting by
the use of the zigzag composition.*

SCENE AT POTTER HEIGHAM (Oils)
This oil painting has a Seagoesque quality, both in subject and composition – not surprising really, as it's Seago's country! The white sails against the distant trees are most effective, seeming to echo the two clouds above. I love the way the trees have been so simply indicated.

39

ROUGH SEA OFF ARRAN (Oils)
There is a very strong tonal pattern about this seascape, which makes it exciting, with its contrasting adjacent lights and darks. The picture is full of movement and vitality, obviously painted quickly, and with great enthusiasm.

UPPINGHAM, THE POST OFFICE
(Watercolour)
Obviously, Ted has used his sharpened matchstick and ink here to capture the detail of this busy scene, albeit loosely. The two pictures on this spread are representative of both ends of Ted's artistic approach.

QUIBERON (Oils)
Here we have a symphony of pinks and greys, the painting being divided into three distinct depths. The buildings on the far distant foreshore are treated with enormous restraint in cool colour, while the detail, texture and warmth have been kept for the foreground rocks.

CLIFTON BRIDGE, BRISTOL (Oils)
Although this painting has been carried out in simple terms, using strong patterns of light and darks, for those of us who know the scene it is unmistakable and evocative of this breathtaking gorge.

GUILDFORD CATHEDRAL FROM THE ROW BARGE (Oils)

This picture gives me a great feeling of satisfaction. The rich variety of greens lends the picture warmth and unity. Notice how the eye is taken along the river and led to the distant cathedral. Although the cathedral is much smaller than the main tree, it attracts attention because it is man-made, and is the only angular object in the whole scene.

St. John's
Blackheath

▽ ROAD TO HOLT, NORFOLK

(Watercolour) *Here Ted has used the classic device of the road, gradually but inevitably leading the eye to the main object of interest – in this case, the grouping of tree, haystack and church. The shadows across the road are also effective, painted as they are with speed and transparency.*

△ HIGH AND DRY (Oils)

There's absolutely no doubt of the main point of interest here; the boat with its strong vertical element, dark tone and the use of the brightest colour, immediately attracts the eye. Note how the distant boat, while not competing, helps to balance the picture. The device of foreground shadow is again used to effect.

◁ AUTUMN LOCK (Watercolour)

There's a beautiful warm glow to this whole scene. The overall autumn colours have been punctuated by the black-and-white posts. Ted has treated the trees with utter simplicity, and has restricted the darks to one central plane.

ROSES (Watercolour)

This is a lovely example of Ted's rose painting as described on page 19. Painted with great simplicity and speed, this is far more evocative than the rather formalised and detailed studies of so many other artists. The simple jamjar in no way detracts from the glory of the flowers.

MISTY MORNING (Watercolour)

This painting could hardly be simpler, and yet is full of atmosphere and delicacy. This is just the kind of scene that Ted loved to tackle. So modest, and yet showing the whole magic of watercolour, with its transparency and subtlety.

SILVERDALE, LANCS (Watercolour)
The main theme of this picture is the quality of light which he has managed to capture on the water. The foreground was obviously cluttered, but Ted has simplified it, while retaining the texture. The background hills have again been reduced to simple flat washes.

MISTY MORNING ON THE RIVER (Oils)
Although painted in oils, this has some of the ethereal quality of watercolour. Ted has achieved the enormous depth of field by the use of warm and cool greens. Notice how the two cows, although tiny in relation to the whole picture, attract the eye immediately. To make sure, Ted seems to have pointed to them with the two lower branches.

NORTH WALES (Watercolour)
This painting would repay long study, especially in the way that Ted has handled the rocks in such a simple yet effective manner. They have been given great strength and stability. The three layers of depth have been clearly defined — a very satisfying picture.

FOUNTAINS
ABBEY, YORKS.

NORFOLK LANDSCAPE (Oils)

Ted has achieved here a really dramatic picture from a simple scene. The main object is the strong, dark tree against the light sky; because of its shape and tone, it pushes the other tree into playing a supportive role. I like too, the really warm foreground, contrasting with the cool blue of the distant hills.

54

BLOWN ROSES (Oils)

If you try covering up the fallen petals in the right-hand bottom corner, you will see how important they are in enlivening the composition. Again we see the humble jamjar used to emphasise the beauty and texture of the flowers, which are thrown into relief by the dark foliage. He loved this picture, and never wanted to sell it; he never did.

ALBURY HEATH (Watercolour)

Most of us would not even notice this scene, and yet Ted has managed to produce a delicate watercolour. The calligraphy of the main tree is beautifully contrasted with the pearly purity of the sky, which in turn is emphasised by the dark, textural quality of the foreground.

56

FRIDAY STREET, SURREY (Oils)
Here we have a symphony of warm and cool greens used to great effect to give distance. It must have been a very still day judging by the strong reflections, and the surface of the river has an almost oily sheen to it, which adds to the illusion.

YARMOUTH HARBOUR, ISLE OF WIGHT (Watercolour)
This is a sky picture in all its limpid glory, occupying three-quarters of the painting. However, the harbour scene with its strongly contrasting darks and lights, provides an exciting foil. Notice how the masts help to unify the two elements.

CONSTANTINE BAY, NEAR NEWQUAY
(Watercolour)
A complete contrast here in weather conditions to the painting opposite. This happy, summer scene is full of depth and activity. The effect of depth has been achieved by the cool blues of the distant horizon, as opposed to the strong red colours of the foreground figures.

SNOW ON MERROW DOWNS (Oils)
Although Ted has not used impasto, his effective use of light and shade on the snow achieves the same effect. Because of the strong shadow, the picture looks sunny, even though the sky is overcast – a very clever painting.

ELY (Watercolour)
Ted has achieved tremendous sparkle here by
his clever use of the paper itself, on the roofs of
the cathedral, adjacent to the very dark trees.
The use of the foreground river with its
reflections, has also enhanced the composition.

BLYTHBOROUGH CHURCH, SUFFOLK
(Watercolour)
*There's a real feeling of Wesson magic here –
watercolour at its most transparent. There are
some beautiful wet into wet passages,
contrasting with the sharp silhouette of the
church. The economy of stroke and elimination
of detail looks so very logical in the finished
painting, yet is so difficult to achieve.*

SNOWDONIA FROM PORT MADOC

(Watercolour)

This is another favourite Wesson type of scene. He knew so well how to portray the depth of field and overall space by the use of simple, economical watercolour washes. Notice the way he's covered the top of the distant mountain with a cloud, adding to the grandeur.

MALDON, ESSEX (Oils)
A lovely composition this, showing clever use of sunshine and shade. Although the barge is obviously the main object of interest, the eye is also drawn to the contrasting patch of sunlit water and sail.

MONT ST MICHEL (Watercolour)
*A very fresh and delicate watercolour,
portraying the famous Brittany scene. Although
the main object of interest is in the middle
distance, the beach is brought forward by the
use of warm pinks. Notice too, how the figures
add scale.*

WINTER TREES, NEAR OVING (Oils)
This is my favourite oil painting, so much so, that I had to have it on the back of the dust jacket. The sky positively glows with light behind the stark winter trees, both being reflected in the waterlogged foreground field. The small tree on the left is important to the balance of the picture.

THE DOULTON VASE (Oils)

This is a really joyous painting, full of bright colour and contrast. It is almost possible to feel the texture of the pot itself. The background has been kept neutral deliberately to give the flowers themselves prominence.

XVI century Tower
Penmarc'h. Finistère

WAXHAM BEACH (Oils)
This painting is full of light and airy space. The foreground has been subtly shaded to take the eye into the middle distance, with its sunlit activity and sparkle. The little pool with its reflected children is also very effective.

THE NEW ROAD TO FORT VICTORIA,
YARMOUTH, ISLE OF WIGHT
(Watercolour)
This is a painting of strong contrasts, being stark, with no attempt at subtlety. The dark trees are counterchanged against the light sky – altogether an arresting picture.

WHERRY AT WEST SOMERTON
(Watercolour)
These boats, with their huge brown sails and telegraph-pole-like masts are, unfortunately, fast disappearing from the Norfolk Broads. Both the sky and the water have been treated with great simplicity, and only the pleasure craft has been given any detail.

BEN NEVIS (Oils)
Although the sunlit mountain dominates the whole painting, it has been made to recede by the rich warm colour of the foreground trees. The lake, though effective, has been treated with great economy.

VENICE FROM GONDOLA STATION
(Watercolour)
This gives the appearance of early morning on the Grand Canal. The profile of the city is simply, but accurately portrayed with a flat wash, while the richness and contrast is reserved for the foreground gondolas. It is unusual and refreshing for Venice to be depicted with such restraint of colour.

SKYE (Watercolour)
There is tremendous depth of field in this calm and relaxed painting. It has obviously been painted at low tide, the flat pink sand contrasting well with the surrounding rocks and their strong colours and textures.

SUNNY LANE NEAR EVERSHOT
(Watercolour)

A hugely effective picture, dominated by the beautiful foreground tree. The shadows across the road, and hedges, provide a good firm base, as well as giving a sunlit quality. Notice how the background trees have been loosely indicated with soft, cool washes, while the various posts add depth.

74

WALBERSWICK (Watercolour)
*This is a scene I know well, as I attended a
painting course of Ted's on this very spot. There
is a very refreshing colour scheme of greens and
blues, with one of the characteristic
Walberswick huts being the main object of
interest – happy memories!*

NEAR EVERSHOT, DORSET (Watercolour)
*Ted could never resist the stark outline of a
good winter tree. One could almost imagine the
squeal of brakes as he pulled up, having seen
this composition from his car. It's interesting to
see how he has treated the telegraph poles, light
against dark, and dark against light, as they
meet the sky.*

CHAPEL, ETON COLLEGE (Oils)
A joyous picture this, with the chapel sparkling in the sunlight. The trees have been kept subdued in value so as not to distract from the excitement of the towers; this is a good example of what can be achieved by putting darkest dark against lightest light.

BLAKENEY CHURCH FROM MORSTON QUAY (Watercolour)
Let's face it, this is a bleak scene. Bleak as only the east coast can be. Ted, however, has managed to evoke its unique character. Look at the subtle colours of the mud, and the way the water reflects the pearly sky.

ETON COLLEGE (Watercolour)

This is one of Ted's rare interiors. Again there is a superb quality of light about it, and I love the way he has varied the colours of the stonework. The white paper has again been used to great effect above the lamp.

ON THE WEY, NEAR GUILDFORD (Oils)

As befits a snow scene, the colours in this tranquil scene are predominantly cool. However, there are touches of warmth in both the grass and the trees, which help to balance the colour scheme. This is a classic composition, with the eye drawn along the river bank towards the main object of interest, in this case, the tree.

SEA PALLING, WAXHAM (Watercolour)
I love the strong, vigorous way the sand dunes in the foreground have been handled, with warm, rich shadows and bold strokes of the mop. The distant church and village have been indicated with great economy, the lights on the church roof have been given great importance – and just look at that lovely limpid sky!

BRANCASTER STAITHE (Watercolour)
This picture is absolutely crammed with interest, with many things competing for attention. However, the eye is immediately drawn to the blue boat, the only cool colour in a predominantly warm painting. The shadows coming from the left-hand corner also point to it.

SEVERN BRIDGE (Watercolour)
This is a very familiar scene to me; I see it every day as I live only a mile from the far side of the bridge, yet the feeling of light and space never ceases to inspire me. Ted has captured the feeling perfectly. There is a vast difference in tone and temperature in his handling of the two banks of the river, which emphasises the depth of field.

STOKE MILL (Oils)
The artist has captured the particular atmosphere of this part of East Anglia; because of the flatness, the sky seems always to dominate the scene. The simple way in which the cattle have been indicated is a good lesson in itself, and just look at that distant church, which gives depth to the picture.

WINTER IN THE GARDEN (Oils)

This was one of Ted's favourite little oils, which was on the walls of his own home; it's always a good sign when an artist doesn't want to let a picture go. There is a variety of colour in the foliage, with the inevitable patch of warmth. Notice how the birds help to balance up the picture.

THAMES MOORING (Watercolour)

The cool blue of the left-hand boat both complements and is a good foil to the autumnal tones in the rest of this picture. I always enjoy studying the way Ted indicates his trees with simplicity, and yet with authenticity – a difficult balance to achieve.

POTTER HEIGHAM (Oils)

The feeling that this is a Norfolk scene is apparent without looking at the title. It was the starting point for dozens of sailing holidays when my family was young. The threatening sky looks familiar too! I love the tiny white sails, so typical of the landscape in that area.

85

CUMBRIAN FORTIFIED FARM
(Watercolour)

This is a good lesson in how to handle apparently flat, grey stones. Ted has managed to get a variety of subtle colour into the surfaces, creating interest and texture. The hens too, indicated very simply, enliven this farmyard scene.

PEMBROKESHIRE COAST NEAR
FISHGUARD (Oils)

This is a wonderful example of Ted's skill with oil painting, and to me is an utterly satisfying picture, having both depth, strength and texture. Predominantly in greys, he has allowed himself an area of warm greens in the left foreground. The two figures on the cliff path are beautifully indicated to give scale.

BAMBURGH CASTLE,
NORTHUMBERLAND (Watercolour)
It is surprising how water seems to creep into such a high proportion of Ted's paintings, but he does handle it so well. He has allowed the very strong profile of the castle to predominate against the light sky, leaving little need for light and shade. Again the foreground rocks are handled with great skill.

BEACH SCENE IN ESSEX (Oils)

Because the foreground beach has been painted in strong, and yet sombre tones, the sky appears positively to glow with light. The beached barge is nicely balanced by the patch of blue. The sails, although tiny, are a very important part of the picture – it wouldn't be nearly as attractive without them.

POLPERRO (Watercolour)

The two pictures on this spread, emphasise the essential qualities, and differences, of watercolour and oil painting. This Cornish landscape is full of lightness and transparency, and positively sparkles. The shadow in the foreground pushes the eye into the sunlit, middle distance, where most of the life and activity take place. Notice how the distant hill sets off the profile of the town.

LOOKING TOWARDS YARMOUTH
FROM CAUSEWAY AT FRESHWATER
(Watercolour)
*This watercolour has a lovely limpid quality,
so typical of Ted. It's so transparent, that the
paper seems to glow through the washes. This
was a quality which he continually tried to
achieve in his watercolours.*

WINTER (Oils)

Again, in contrast to the opposite page, this picture has enormous strength and power. The paint, being thickly applied, particularly in the foreground hedge, makes you want to touch it, as well as making you want to pull your collar up around your ears.

ABEL FLETCHER'S MILL,
TEWKESBURY (Watercolour)
*This was one of Ted's favourite mills (I own
another version of it myself). I love this limpid
sky with the flicks of white. The river is really*
*'wet', painted quickly and with assurance.
There are some lovely warm colours in the
various buildings. The detail and contrast on
the sluice gate make it the main object of
interest.*

CHICHESTER CANAL (Watercolour)
What makes this picture so attractive to me is the way in which the reflections in the water have been handled – they are almost perfect. Notice too, how the picture divides into three layers of depth, from the cool blues of the distant hills, the cool greens of the mid-distance trees and the warm rich colours of the canal bank. There is a lot to learn from this picture.

WINTER SPORT AT NEWLANDS CORNER (Watercolour)

Of this painting Ted said, 'Here, on one of Surrey's well-known beauty spots, we see the wonderful effect of a fall of snow, how it changes the values and the importance of commonplace scenes, putting the emphasis on details which we would normally take for granted'. Although the children and their toboggan were the focal point, the main point of interest surely, was the very dark group of trees against an almost non-existent view of the North Downs, beyond.

AUTUMN BUNCH (Oils)
There is a lesson here in the way Ted has kept the background, including the jamjar, monochromatic, so that the whole emphasis and glory is reserved for the flowers. Furthermore, because of its strength and colour, he has made one flower more important than the rest, and the eye is immediately drawn to its richness.

ST AUBIN JERSEY (Watercolour)
This simple, delicate painting shows a superb purity of wash, which was one of Ted's unique achievements. It has the atmosphere of a quiet sunny morning, with nothing to disturb the peace and tranquillity of this idyllic spot.

HORSEY MILL, NORFOLK (Watercolour)
Until you have tried painting windmills yourself, you don't realise how tremendously difficult it is to portray the sails with delicacy and economy, as they are here. There are many examples of failed attempts. They are a very tempting subject, almost to the point of being a cliché. Notice how the shadow of the sail on the building helps to describe its shape.

99

WHITE SANDS OF MORAR (Watercolour)

At the risk of overstating the case, just look at the way Ted has put on his washes with directness and transparency. You will never find any fiddling or muddiness in his work. I feel that every would-be watercolourist should strive for this quality, even though many of us never achieve it.

WINTER WILLOWS AT PEASMARSH
(Watercolour)

A hugely enjoyable painting this, the sort of simple subject that Ted enjoyed tackling. It suited his style and approach beautifully. Notice how he has lightened the foreground tree just at the point where it crosses the one behind, so separating them. Also, how important the shadows are in conveying the contours of the ground beneath.

101

RIVER ARUN, NEAR BLACKRABBIT
(Watercolour)

The clarity of the water and sky scene below cried out for watercolour medium, whereas the subject opposite was just as obviously more suited to oils. This is a picture of alternating warms and cools. Look how Ted has made no attempt to add ripples so beloved of many amateur artists, but has let the simple wash speak for itself.

PORTLAND BILL (Oils)

Ted has captured the dazzling brilliance of the sunshine on the rocks, especially in the foreground. Notice how the range of contrasts has been narrowed as the picture recedes to the horizon. Also, the greens have changed in temperature to emphasise the depth of field of the painting. The underwater rocks add a further quality.

SIDLESHAM QUAY (Line and Wash)
This is an example of Ted's line and wash technique, where he has indicated some of the architectural details with, probably, a sharpened matchstick dipped in waterproof ink. However, for the rest of the painting, he has used pure watercolour. The warm tree on the right pushes the cool tree, behind the figures, further into the background.

NORTH DOWNS, NEWLANDS CORNER
(Oils)
Amazingly, there is a feeling of warmth and sunshine in what is predominantly a cool painting. The quality of the snow is beautiful, the footprints adding a third dimension. The shadows on the snow are inevitably blue as they reflect the sky above. I love the touch of calligraphy in the two distant saplings.

KYLE OF TONGUE, BEN LOYAL
(Watercolour)

This painting has a mystical quality and could only be in Scotland; again the subject lends itself to watercolour. Ted has shown enormous restraint in the way he has portrayed the loch, and the foreground pools. Not one single stroke has been wasted. No one could have handled this subject with less brevity, or more assurance I also love the touch of wet into wet on the far distant Ben Loyal.

107

ST MICHAEL'S MOUNT, CORNWALL
(Watercolour)

What a feeling of peace and quiet the artist has captured here. I can't use the phrase 'limpid washes' again, but just look at it! The profile of the mount stands out strong and sturdy amidst the ethereal atmosphere of the rest of the painting. The birds are a masterly touch which he keeps in reserve for an occasion such as this.

PORTLAND FROM OSMINGTON
(Watercolour)

In contrast to the painting opposite, this is a far busier subject, handled with confidence. There is plenty of sparkling counterchange amid the boats and huts, which is very entertaining. See how Ted has reduced the huts to simple but dramatic shapes, resisting the temptation many of us have, to elaborate and overwork.

108

INCOMING TIDE, FRESHWATER (Oils)
This is a strong L-shaped composition, and Ted has used the device of darkening the foreground tones to dramatise deliberately the white foam against it, which is almost dazzling.

Although the foreground is dark, it has lots of bounced light in it. This is something which is often neglected by amateur painters.

110

FARMYARD BEHIND YARMOUTH, ISLE OF WIGHT (Watercolour)

The design of this picture has been really well thought out, and Ted has used several devices to make the tall building the main object of interest. First, it is counterchanged sharply against the dark trees, second, the roof is the brightest colour in the whole picture, and third, the shadow coming in from the right foreground points to it.

BROWNSEA ISLAND (Watercolour)
This an object lesson on tackling a large panorama, which stretches back miles. He keeps up the excitement of counterchanging one layer against the next, back into the distance. Brownsea Island is famous for being the site of the first Boy Scout camp set up by Baden Powell.

BRIDGE AT KIRKBY LONSDALE
(Watercolour)

This bridge has been painted by many famous artists including Roland Hilder, and lends itself to dramatic treatment. The strong architecture is surrounded by masses of foliage, like a brilliant jewel on a velvet cushion. It's a free, loose painting, even by Wesson's standards, and has worked beautifully.

▷ MALLAIG, SKYE FERRY
Although it is small in relation to the rest of the painting, the eye is immediately drawn to the black and white ferry, which stands out against the threatening and dominant sky. The cool, subtle grey-greens of the sea give way to the rich darks of the distant hills, providing depth in this exciting painting.

◁ ROSES (Oils)
This is a tiny painting carried out in a loving and tender way. Ted did, after all, have a soft spot for roses, and couldn't bear to part with this particular work. He has somehow managed to combine strong, thrusting brush strokes with incredible delicacy, which would seem to be an impossibility, but he's done it!

▷ CHICHESTER CATHEDRAL (Watercolour)
You can see this cathedral spire for miles around, owing to the flatness of the area between the downs and the sea. Again, Ted has used the device of making the bottom third subdued and dark, in order to throw up the brilliance of the sky. This is also emphasised by touches of white paper on the roofs representing light reflected from the sky.

STILL LIFE (Oils)
This is an unusual departure for Ted, as apart from his flower paintings, he preferred to work outside. The eye is first attracted to the middle orange, because of the way it is counterchanged against the dark bottle. The strong colour scheme is extremely effective, as the orange is complementary to the greens.

WYLYE VALLEY IN SNOW (Watercolour)
What could be in greater contrast to the painting on the opposite page, than this joyfully executed watercolour? It would pay any watercolourist to make a study of these winter trees; he has got the effect of the twigs by using lightning sideways strokes with his mop barely touching the paper – so simple and yet so effective.

117

WHITWORTH, DEVON (Line and wash)

There's a lovely overall warmth about this painting. Look where Ted has left the paper untouched for the white houses. The line work was probably done with a sharpened matchstick, and as usual with this technique he's kept his colours very restricted. Note also the old trick of the shadow across the foreground street to hold the picture together and provide a base.

SHERE, SURREY (Watercolour)
Ted has achieved a great feeling of depth in this painting, by using very cool pale blue for the distant hills and warm, rich ocres and browns for the foreground. Note the way he has changed the angles of the trees to avoid monotony.

QUINAG (Oils)

This painting absolutely glows with subtle colour. The cool blue of the loch is surrounded by beautifully warm pinks and mauves which give a real feeling of satisfaction to the viewer. There's a grandeur and solidity to the painting which is breathtaking.

PREPARING FOR DINGHY RACE
(Watercolour)

This is another of Ted's favourite subjects, and there are in existence several variations of this, or similar scenes. It portrays the excitement leading up to the start of a race, in this case a Fireball class. Notice how he has kept nearly all the activity and contrast to one tiny part of the painting, leaving the rest in a supportive role.

LOOKING TOWARDS WYLYE (Oils)

This was probably done as a demonstration to his eager students, as it is quite near to Philipps House at Dinton, where Ted ran several courses each year. Again, it is a good example of the way the greens are subdued and greyed down as the picture recedes. The single red roof is also very effective.

WINTER PUDDLES (Watercolour)

Just look at these beautifully handled winter trees. Not a stroke is wasted and there is so little detail. The sparse foliage is merely hinted at. Notice how the puddles have been placed in just the right place to reflect the two posts behind them, giving the effect of water. The sky too is magnificent.

WALBERSWICK FROM SOUTHWOLD
(Watercolour)

This high-key watercolour has so much of the atmosphere of the East Anglian location where I had the pleasure of painting under Ted's guidance. He has treated the scene with restraint, resisting the temptation to paint too many darks, thus retaining the soft light.

NEW FOREST (Oils)

The counterchange which Ted has used, putting the lightest part of the sky directly behind the darkest trees, has produced a painting full of mood and drama. The sky itself is full of movement, and is given extra brilliance by the contrast of the dark foreground.

SNOWDONIA FROM PORT MADOC
(Oils)

Isn't this fabulous? One can imagine the enthusiasm Ted must have been feeling as he painted the grandeur of this Welsh mountain and its reflection in the estuary below. I love the way he has portrayed Snowdon in a symphony of pinks and mauves, and it is interesting to compare this with the watercolour of the same scene on page 62. Incidentally, Dickie told me that these were painted from a rubbish dump!

126

ON THE MOLE, NEAR WOKING (Oils)
Although this painting has no detail whatsoever, Ted has managed to render a wonderful variety of foliage. It could have been so flat, but instead there is enormous richness and shape. The reflections too have been beautifully handled, and complete the scene.

STILL LIFE WITH PRAWNS (Oils)
Ted didn't often paint still lifes, but this painting has colour, charm and balance. The predominantly grey background complements the pinks of the prawns beautifully, and the various directions of the tails give a sense of movement almost like a Catherine wheel.

THE LANE IN SUMMER (Oils)
This is an unusual painting for Ted, both in subject and approach. It has the freshness and sunny quality of the French Impressionists. The shadows play an important part here in giving the picture warmth. The red chimneys also attract the eye immediately, and provide contrast and impact.

Index

Numbers in **bold** indicate illustrations or captions